goodbye innocence, hello desires

Rebeca Cozma

BookLeaf Publishing

India | USA | UK

Presentation by *BookLeaf Publishing*

Web: www.bookleafpub.com

E-mail: info@bookleafpub.com

ISBN: 9789358314229

First edition 2023

To those who hesitate to follow their desires.

It is not easy, but as long as it is legal, go for it!

Trigger warning

Some poems contain explicit content not
suitable for children, including depictions of sex
and acts of violence.

Table of Contents

the dare

I'll let you catch me,
If I fall head over heels for you.
I'll take your dare, and I'll let go of my doubts,
For I want to trust you.

I have been hurt before, I have been let down.
Yet, somehow you feel so right.
I'll take a chance, I'll stick around,
And see where this love takes us for now.

It won't be easy,
To break through my defences,
But I'm willing to take the risk,
And see where our love begins.

So dare me to love you.
I'll take the challenge,
For I know that with you by my side,
My heart will find some balance.

I'll take your dare,
Let myself fall.
Perhaps with you,
I could have it all.

whistling a tune

We clicked at "hi,"
But crashed at "goodbye."
Don't bother coming back.

We're through, I'm over you.
We're through, you can only enjoy the view.
We're through, you can wait in the queue.

You couldn't appreciate me when we were
together,
Now you've lost me forever.
It's your loss, baby, not mine.
There's another one waiting for me over the line.
So I'm just fine, sipping on my wine.

I'm over the moon,
Whistling a tune,
'Cause I'm immune
To your bullshit.

Now that you're gone, I can see the dawn.
Now that you're gone, it's a delight to see the
bright daylight.
Now that you're gone, my smile is a
phenomenon.

I was a hopeless romantic, so I took my chances.
Turns out you were a bandit,
Left my love stranded.
When it finally landed, I became enchanted,
Now you can never take me for granted.

I'm over the moon,
Whistling a tune,
'Cause I'm immune
To your bullshit.

delirium

You're notorious for being devious,
Yet, like an idiot, I still find you glorious.
All the other guys are invidious of your
experience,
Such a shame that you're supercilious, just like
Odysseus.

From the way you walk all luxurious,
It's obvious that you're nefarious,
But boy, I'm curious if you're also spontaneous,
'Cause I'll ride you like a Sagittarius!

I'm serious, you send me into delirium,
Need no helium. Period.
It's hilarious how you send me into oblivion for
being mysterious.
You send me into delirium.

Isn't it dangerous, being this flavorous?
Making all heads turn, making all hearts burn.
Just from watching you walk into a room,
I'll gladly jump over the broom, and make you
my groom.

From the way you walk all luxurious,

It's obvious that you're nefarious,
But boy, I'm curious if you're also spontaneous,
'Cause I'll ride you like a Sagittarius!

I'm serious, you send me into delirium,
Need no helium.
Period.

painted whispers

Painted whispers
on these four walls.
Painted whispers
on this king-sized bed.
Painted whispers
on the kitchen counter.

Painted whispers
stained on these sheets.
Painted whispers
lingering in the air.
Painted whispers
stuck to the floors.

Painted whispers
marked on the carpet.
Painted whispers
engraved on this sofa.
Painted whispers
bruised on my neck.

closed eyes

Covered in a satin scarf,
she can't see,
the face he's making with her pleas.

She's alive
from the feathered kisses
trailing along her body.
This has become her newest hobby.

Covered in a satin scarf,
her eyes roll back,
his grunts making her melt all at once.

She's alive,
thrilled from the dive,
thriving under these sheets tonight.

Covered in a satin scarf,
gripping onto satin sheets,
neighbours probably hearing her screams.

She's got her eyes closed,
indulging in his moans.

strangers

She's in a stranger's bed wide open,
mere hours after being heartbroken.

We've never spoken,
communication only through glances,
who gives a fuck about romances?

She's going to enjoy this,
I'm going to ride her into bliss.

It's obvious she's new to this,
but the way I got her rolling,
I'm going to be the only one she's moaning!

The look in her eyes,
begs me not to be nice,
I'll be sure to give her paradise.

She's in a stranger's bed wide open,
mere hours after being heartbroken.

She's in my bed,
laying like a token,
all breathless and broken.

match not made in heaven

Our love, like a pair of matches,
With one wrong move, it will ignite,
Leaving behind scars and scratches,
Yet, I can't help but hold you tight.

We are two sides of the same coin,
They say opposites attract,
But every time we come together,
It's like waiting for fire to erupt.

And as the flame,
Dances and flows,
The flicker grows along with the pain
Of a love we can't let go.

It's a dangerous game we play,
But we can't resist each other's touch,
A burning fire,
That we can't get enough.

turbulence

We were always at odds,
Clashing over words,
Shouting over looks,
Crying over gestures.

We were always at odds,
Yet,
We found each other
And clung to one another.

On the days I hate you,
I want to run you over with my car
Or fuck you 'til sunlight.

On the days I love you,
I want to hold you tight
And make you mine.

It's those days that last the least
Because somehow you find a way to anger me,
And,
We're once again at odds.

Threatening each other with knives,
Hatred radiating from our eyes.

Neck to neck, close enough to kill,
But something softens in your eyes.

And, once again,
We make up in bed,
Preparing to create a different kind of mess.

stopwatch & hourglass

Stopwatch,
Hourglass,
Stopping time to realise how bad you were for
me.

People were right from the start,
We were never meant to be.
But baby, at the time,
You were all that I could see.

I never expected you to be like that,
Especially when we've been through hell and
back.
I put my heart out there for you.
All you did was take it, break it, leave it,
And I simply ignored the clues.

One day you left my life.
Not even saying goodbye.
All you did was take your shit and fly.
Then, you come knocking at my door,
Asking to be like we were before.
But I don't need you anymore.

I can assure you,

I no longer adore you.
Go back to your mistress and keep your
distance.
God is my witness that I got you out of my
system,
So hasta la vista!

You thought you could come back, and I
wouldn't bark?
I got my life back on track, and this time, I'm
ready to attack!
You really thought I'd keep my mouth shut?
I said nothing at all when you provoked my
downfall,
What makes you think you can crawl back to
me, and I wouldn't drown you in the Black Sea?

One day you left my life.
Not even saying goodbye.
All you did was take your shit and fly.
Then, you come knocking at my door,
Asking to be like we were before.
But I don't need you anymore.

Yes, I was torn when you said you were done
for,
And left me crying while the other girl waited at
my front door.

Are you here now to implore with your knees on
the floor?
God, that is such an eyesore!
Did you get bored and decided to return?
I suggest you do a half turn,
Because what you do from now on is none of
my concern.

I should have listened to the advice,
That being with you would be a fool's paradise,
Not worth the sacrifice.
I was so blinded,
That I couldn't see your vice,
That I didn't recognise the demise
When you stopped being nice.

I can assure you,
I no longer adore you.
Go back to your mistress and keep your
distance.
God is my witness that I got you out of my
system,
So hasta la vista!

Stopwatch,
Hourglass,
I stopped time, and realised, how fucked up you
were.

dalliance

Our short-lived dalliance,
It was instantaneous,
Lacked resilience.
Fuelled by lust,
Burned to dust.

He wanted to keep everything hushed,
But a bitter feeling deep within me,
Forces me to reveal,
The cruelty he wanted to conceal.

Whispers under the moonlight,
Melting under bedsheets at night,
Floating from all the delight.
I must have lost all my foresight,
For I did not expect a feeling so right to be
My plight.

That demure housewife of his, the
simple-minded fool,
Had no idea how quickly he came to life when
playing
With that pocket-knife,
With me on all fours,
Her,

Stuck inside four walls.

Or was I the fool?
For laughing, smiling,
When he showed cruelty, as if it would
miraculously
Become love and not promiscuity.
As if all the jewellery justified his lust
For my bloodshed on that damned scarlet bed.

When my screams no longer sufficed,
When my blood could no longer incite,
He replaced the knife with the gun,
The thigh with the forehead,
And whispered, "We're done," as his finger
touched the trigger.

But, like a phoenix rising from the ashes,
I returned to leave scratches.
I returned to reciprocate the bloodshed.
One of us has to be dead!

So, I took the final step and...

I killed him.
I slashed his throat in front of
His beloved wife.
I slashed his throat and ended
His lavished life.

I killed him.
I slashed his throat and
Bathed in his blood.
I slashed his throat for the
Memories he said he loved.

Cheers to our short-lived dalliance!

ruined touch

I lay on a crimson bed,
Drenched from the words you said.
One more kiss,
Until pure bliss hits.
One more touch,
Until it feels too much.

I spend nights wide awake,
Reminiscing the ache, your ability to make me
quake.
One more thought,
And I'll be once again in your yacht,
Asking you to give me all you've got.
One more touch,
And I'm sure you'll forget about her.

I glance at my phone, waiting for your calls,
Waiting for me to be your spur-of-the-moment
one more time.
Hoping your girlfriend doesn't notice my
anxious eyes
As I give her a smile,
While plotting how to make you mine.

I lay on a crimson bed,

Drenched from the words she said.
Her last word,
Sounded like a broken chord.
Her last word,
Barely heard.

A plea, *Please*,
Like the one you used to whisper,
When you asked me to keep us a secret.
But you know what?
For every call you ignored,
She got a deep cut.
It was thrilling to see I was the one she feared.
Her makeup smeared,
Like mine was
When you said us being together was absurd.

I was only good enough when
You got hard.
But the moment I wanted more,
I was so easy to discard.
You know what else was easy?
Making your girlfriend,
Sorry, my mistake, *your ex*,
End up in a graveyard.

Your last touch,
It was too much.
You shouldn't have gripped my throat and

Laughed as I choked.
Waited for my eyes to close,
Before you left, oh so grandiose,
Thinking it was adios.

Boy, were you wrong!
That night wasn't *"so long."*
A piece of advice, next time make sure I can't
come back,
Because right now,
My return comes with a thirst for more blood.

I lay on a crimson bed,
Drenched from the words you said.
Your last word,
Was that dreaded plea, *Please*,
Like the one you used to whisper,
When you asked me to keep us a secret.

Your last touch,
Ruined us.

tarnished reign

Your reign thrived on my pain.
Your crown silenced my ability to complain.
Always by your side, constrained and tied,
Forced to abide and sing your praise,
As if you possessed heavenly power,
When I was merely a sunflower,
Bound by my need to survive off your light.
Knowing this, you radiated with delight.

I am your saviour, you know that, dear.
There's no need to fear me, is that clear?

I put you on a pedestal, and you became
insatiable.
You saw yourself as the emperor of an empire
taken by force.
Before you came along, I might have been lost,
But at least I still knew myself.
This realm of mine needed help, and you simply
took it for yourself,
And along with the land, you took my hand.

I tell you what you can and cannot do because I
love you.

*And if you love me, you won't dare disagree, but
you are free to get on your knees and plead.*

You arrived disguised as an angel, hiding your
hatred.
Instead, you were the devil, took my hand to
feed off my vessel,
Ensuring my life would be marked by pain and
shame,
Because you flourished in this game,
While I rotted into something easily forgotten.
You might have won the first round, but there is
something you couldn't fathom,
That I can blossom from the ground.

*I only wanted what was best for you, and you
knew.
Please, dear, this is not something you need to
do.*

A tarnished reign I have created from the
vengeance that clouded my gaze.
In this game of spades, I threw grenades,
For your vicious ways to forever desiccate.
You wanted to completely ruin me, to corrupt
me,
But you failed to realise that naivety will never
get the best of me,

That foolishness is something I refuse to
succumb to.
With a move towards your ruin, I paved my
path,
Towards a legacy that will last.

In this tarnished reign, I rebuilt my realm.

mayhem

Mayhem against him,
For the pain he sought to inflict in me,
For the tears that flowed endlessly.
Mayhem against the smug look on his face,
Mayhem shall unleash in this place.

I will not stand idly by,
As he thrives every time he sees me cry.
I will fight with all my might
And bring him down with all my sight.
Mayhem shall be his blight.

Mayhem against him,
For the hurt he tried to bring,
For the sorrow I refuse to feel any longer.
Mayhem against the fears he tried to enforce,
Mayhem shall unleash its force.

I will not let him win.
I will not watch him grin, thinking victory is his.
I will stand tall
And show him where he belongs,
Six feet underground, nothing left of him but a
rotting corpse.

Mayhem shall be unleashed on everyone that
dares to mourn.

recapture

Struck by hunger,
Struck by anger,
We commence our fight to conquer.
It's about time someone killed
That murderous old man.

Fuelled by starvation,
Fuelled by exploitation,
We begin our battle towards freedom.
It's time we mislead him,
For he deserves to stop breathing.

Tired of barbarity,
Tired of disparity,
We're simply seeking clarity.
So, we ride at dawn,
We break down doors,
We start wars,
For all the cries he ignores.

Seeking justice,
Seeking death,
We want him to have the same end as Macbeth.
For all the power and control he sought,
We commence the assault on his court.

We regain the control that should have been ours
by default.

insubordination

Since when is having a voice
An insubordination?
Since when is having emotions
A transgression?

I guess, it's when my actions,
As a woman,
Seemingly pose a threat to a
Sensitive patriarchy,
Ruled by those with a
Fragile masculinity,
Unable to handle the possibility of
Gender symmetry,
Unable to let go of a
Chauvinistic hierarchy.

Insubordination?
More like keeping us in check,
Riveting in our wreck.
Insubordination?
An accusation to continue your manipulation.
Insubordination?
No. We're breaking free from sexist
machination.

You don't like my tone?
Says the man that condones oppression.
Says the man that attempts to eliminate
Female expression.
Says the man unable to accept progression.

Since when is having a voice
An insubordination?
Since when is having emotions
A transgression?

I'm too emotional according to you,
Incapable to rule,
Proceedings guided by feelings.
Coming from the man that,
Resorts to violence while
Remaining camouflaged under the image of
being pious.

Insubordination?
For wanting body autonomy.
Insubordination?
For wanting equality.

It's not insubordination.
It's your inability to let go of a
Fixation on the past.
Because once that's gone,
How long can your power last?

life locked in glass

Another petal has fallen.
Another piece of the flower broken.
We gave everything for a chance to bloom.
Instead,
We found ourselves sombre and numb,
Withering
Into nothing,
Because no matter how much we give,
It will never be enough.

Another petal has fallen.
Confined within a crystal glass,
Only one more petal stands.
How long do you think it will last?
In theory, we could survive
(with a little sun and water),
But knowing reality, the glass will be
Smashed in two,
Before we have the chance,
To make it through.

The last petal has fallen.
Surrounded by shards of broken glass,
Everything seems to be against us.
Why?

The centuries before didn't suffice?
We were the ones who paid the price for your
Inability to grant us rights.

The last petal has fallen.
Discarded and disregarded.
But who cares, right?
Our voices silenced, no one to heed our cries,
Deprived of the freedom to decide.
Pushed from one state to another,
Just for the chance to choose our own lives
without
Persecution.

We are asking, muffled by the ground,
For society's retribution.

learned her lesson

She was drinking at the time,
Never expecting that night.
The pain and guilt—
Is this how it feels to be the victim?
The judgments and blame—
Is this how it feels to be a woman?

He was drinking at the time,
Knowing exactly what he wanted that night.
The excuses, justifications—
Is this how it feels to be believed?
"He didn't know what he was doing."—
Really? Is this how it feels to be a man?

She was told,
"Relax and enjoy.
It's going to happen anyway."
She was told,
"Lay still and be quiet.
You're screaming when you should be
compliant."

He shrugged and said to his friends,
"I just wanted to have some fun.

*Why is she suddenly acting like a nun? She
certainly wasn't dressed like one."*
He simply stated,
*"It was good for my soul,
Having that kind of control."*

She was silenced,
For that's when a woman is at her finest.
She was told that being defiant wasn't the
wisest.
For a woman's voice should remain confined,
Ideally resigned into darkness,
As if nothing ever happened.

He was acquitted,
For how can a man be found guilty,
When her state of mind made her willing?
He was forgiven,
For how can a man in society be accused,
When he was in a state of inebriety?

roles reversed

Let's reverse our roles,
For words seem to be continuously ignored.
As if a woman opening her mouth,
Can only be tolerated if giving pleasure to a
man.

Let's reverse our roles,
Because every attempt to be heard,
Has been classified as absurd.

You would think that after centuries,
We would no longer be seen as mere
accessories.
And every attempt to vocalise this,
Has been twisted to make us appear as the
enemy.

So, let's reverse our roles,

Let's say that we have the upper hand, and that
you,
As a man,
Are subjected to what we are on a daily basis.
Let's see how you would feel being controlled,
criticised, condemned

For simply existing.

First,
You have feelings, but because you have a dick,
they will be cast aside.
For all we care about is how it can be used to
give us a joyride.
But you're hearing this and thinking, *"I don't
see how that's a problem."*

Predictable.

Yet, would the joy still be there,
If taken by force?
No matter how much you cried?
No matter how scared?

"Well, just say no."

Say no? As if it means anything coming from
someone with a dick.
Say no? When you look and dress as if you're
asking for it?

Say no? You shouldn't have been walking down
the street, exposing your shoulders and legs.
Say no? You shouldn't have been drinking,
going out with friends.

Say no? When it seems to be synonymous with
consent?
Say no? As if it holds any power.

Is this hurting your feelings?
I don't care much for them.
And when I do consider them, I will simply
ignore them.
You're just being too emotional. Irrational.
There's no reason for you to be frustrated and
angry.
I will dismiss them as unimportant.
Mere delusions.

As a woman, I know better.
So, second, you have a voice.
But since it's only acknowledged when it
signifies feeling high from all the riding, you
know,
Moaning and asking for more,
Outside of that, it is perfectly fine to be ignored.

Oh, you've decided to use it to demand for equal
pay?
You're asking to be heard and seen as an actual
human being?
That cannot be right!
You were built to obey.
You are not meant to have opinions.

Since it is causing such an uproar, fine, I'll bite.
I will pretend to listen, I'll feign concern and
sympathy.
I might even give in and grant you some
freedom.

You're happy now, right?

Now that I have acknowledged the inequality,
But have no intention of doing anything about it.
Because giving you power will diminish mine.
Because I fear that increasing your autonomy
will lead to an insurrection,
To my displacement.

Are you angry?
Protesting your rights?
How can you do this!?
We have given you so much!
How dare you be ungrateful!

We may have the same jobs, sure, I may earn
more, but as a woman, I deserve it.
I am mentally and emotionally stronger, capable
of making rational decisions.
I am qualified to be in a position of power.
You don't have what it takes to climb this
hierarchy.

Why are you trying to change the social order?
The audacity of you thinking you would stand a
chance!
Just because I granted you some freedom, does
not mean you should use it.

So, would words still be continuously ignored,
If our roles were reversed?

9 789358 314229